Bokeh, the hues within

Gayatri Lekshmy Kumar

A collection of poems

WRITERS' READERS

Published by Booksthakam, India
info@booksthakam.com
www.booksthakam.com

Bokeh, the hues within : A collection of poems

A Booksthakam Book/ published by arrangement with the author

ISBN: 978-93-94378-37-7

Typeset and Cover Design by Cogitabund LLP
Printed and bounded in India by Manipal Technologies Limited

FSC www.fsc.org MIX Paper | Supporting responsible forestry FSC® C043100

Contents

To the unseen magic around me,
some day we shall meet face to face.

Acknowledgement

My pen quivers at the enormous list of names that I bow in gratitude to, right from my childhood unto now.

For those who etched a golden calligraphy of memories into my heart, I remain ever so grateful unto the end.

For those who made me go through pain and suffering, iam thankful for the lessons learnt.

For the beautiful and magical nature that has often healed me and left me speechless with its gentle touch and magnanimity, I bow in gratitude.

To my readers and friends who have always inspired me to write more and more, here's my gift to you.

My dear family and soul mates who made me who I am and stood steadfast by my side, I hold close to my heart.

And to my kids, my elixir of joy and hope, I love you very much.

Foreword

Poetry, to me, has always been a means to speak aloud the hidden whispers of my heart. Some moments in life when prose is too weary an attempt to give words to the hearts chatter.Each poem is a cloud drifting aimlessly in the cosmos of my mind. It is interspersed by comets that aim to quench the rebel in me.

These pages hold joy and pain, memories and desires. Some were written in hushed tones while others in the eye of storm. I never wrote with the intention of being understood, only of being honest. And maybe, just out of pure coincidence you may be able to relate to my experiences.

I invite you, my friend, to spend some time here with me. Read at your own pace. Reflect. This book is not a means to an end, but a journey unfolding. And if one line stays with you—lingers like a sigh or memory you can't forget—then I've done justice with my words.

With regards
Gayatri

Bokeh, the hues within

Memory

I have always been told, that I have one,
An owner of a fickle memory,
So inconsistent and flitting,
Yet I remember with love, all those whom I love,
Who loved me as I am, and made me love myself,
I remember with gratitude, those who taught me lessons in life,
To forego retribution, to make allowance,
To forgive and to accept, a human as a whole,
Mistakes and accolades, they go hand in hand,
Maybe I forgot my history and geography lessons,
Maybe I forgot my teacher's words,
Maybe I forgot some of my childhood friends,
Try as hard as I might, some faces, some situations, some words,
Have been erased for eternity,
Yet I know and remember how I felt,
How glad I felt, how grateful,
I'm glad I lived, those years, though not in full,
I regret not, that I couldn't do,
I regret not, that I forgot, because, it was meant to be,
The memories, they were meant to go,
No noose could have held back, that which was destined to go
I live on, creating new ones, and will do so,
As long as I tread in the book of life.

The silent threads of dissent…hush

It's as if the sun is a male, as if the female spirit couldn't shine...
The silent voice of dissent, that echoes in the ears, as she tries out her new outfit...
The silent voice that rebels, as she explores her feminity...
Invisible throes that accompany the lone travelling spirit...
Muted despair, as she gives up her long cherished dreams...
The silent snarls that rebuke the voice that reeks of chauvinism...
Oh, why is it that the female gender needs to feel small joys only after struggles...
It's as if freedom is rebellion, and they say independence is yours ?!!!
Every human wish seems, nay is a struggle in reality...
Oh, for a world where daughters are born free, in the true sense of the word...
Free from the bondage of invisible dissent, free from the mind's prisons...

Stillness amidst chaos

To be aware, of the presence,
It's a cake walk in silence,
Amidst the peace of nature,
Amidst company of like minded souls,
In the heat of passion, doing what you love most,
Amidst carefully curated solitude,
But it seems to have disappeared into thin air,
When it's chaos all around, noise and confusion,
When it's a pell mell, and babbles endless engulf you.
When the continuous bombardment of mind with
inquisitive doubts,
Raised by kids, leaves one fending for silence.
Yet now amidst the chaos, I see myself,
I muse on my responses, livid or ashen,
I see how far I have come, I feel blessed,
I strongly believe in the futility of expectations,
And the necessity to live in the moment,
To be still amidst the chaos, and discern the threads of love,
The silent threads that bind us, you and me in love.

Rape

How hateful a word, a word which must not be named,
When daughters grow up in ignorance,
Of the cruelty they may face,
Isn't it akin to murder or plunder,
Is it possible for a man, a human to do so,
A cruelty of such magnitude,
Enough to kill the soul of the victim,
Either die or take rebirth, a new soul in an old body,
Marred by scars, and years to heal.
Is it lust or pure violence, I wouldn't dare to call it animus,
Animals are so tame and 'human', or I say, 'animal'
Not worth a dime of comparison.
Aren't the roots deep, elite and wretched alike,
If something so beautiful as a union of like minds,
Can evoke painful memories of a bitter bygone past.
Shouldn't the kids know, both boys, girls alike,
The dangers that lurk in unseen haunts,
Shouldn't the boys know that the girls deserve respect,
Dignity and respect for their souls,
That the bodies of girls are private and holy and not public fields of frolic for mania,
That every moment of life, every breath,
Of man or animal is their own,
That tampering may lead to irreparable damage of the individual and nation.
May peace prevail, may minds seek sense,
May the boys grow, to respect and to love.

If I were a patient…

I would wish for a doctor with a lot of empathy.
I wish that I could ask the silliest of doubts, without fear.
I would wish to hear good news every day about my slight and steady recovery.
The dirt and grime on the walls and sundry, dampen my spirits.
With all patience, I wish they were clean and sparkled clean.
I wish the medical fraternity would look into my eyes beyond goggles and face shield.
And address my soul within, in ways that need no words.
When in pain as I moan and groan, look at me not in [1]apathy.
I know how you sweat beneath the garb of white...
Yet, I implore you to shed an ounce of mercy at my hapless soul.
Open the windows so that the sun kisses my cheeks, warm.
I wish to hear the chirping birds and music that can heal...
Let my loved ones be by side for they know what I pine.
I respect you and I'm proud of you, my saviour.
But I wish that you see my tears and how I wish to fly away, healthy and free.

1

Fear of the unknown

Yes, it's true, tomorrow may not exist,
Yes, it's true, my sleep may be eternal,
Yes, it's true, it's not worth it to expect big,
Yes, it's true, people change by the minute,
Yes, it's true, your loved ones are mortal,
Yes, it's true, my children will soon be adults,
Yes, it's true, my desires may come to naught,
But, what a life, is one without hope,
What a life, is one without emotions,
What a life, is one without expectations,
What a life, is one without desires,
For the multitude of emotions, and the,
Highs and lows of life, maketh, life, one good treasure,
So, as long as I live a worldly life, let me be marred and scarred by,
The joys and sorrows all alike.
Let me unabashedly be in love with all that is,
Let me be guilt free in following all that my heart seeks,
For this is one life, that I live.

In my house

In my house are rooms, small and large,
There are corridors, dark and bright,
You my guest, shall be in the living room,
For as long as you please,
There I shall serve you fruits and drink,
And enthuse you with my tall tales,
Yet tread not beyond the hall, my dear,
For in the rooms, I forbid your presence,
I shall let you oh, friend, into my hygge corner,
When I know that you too are my hygge,
I shall let you into my study, oh, friend,
Only if u understand my language, the language of my mind,
And into my bedroom, I shall let you my friend,
Only if I'm safe with you, my mind and body,
When your eyes can see the flower that blooms at night,
Vulnerable and true, tender and pure,
Till then you may loiter in the halls and corridors,
Where lay souls wander, oblivious to the truths,
Till then may my room be locked, away from prying eyes,
Prying eyes, that mean no good.

My dear boy friends

Ease yourself, and take a breath...
Exhale the insecurities that bind you...
Break the norm to be a stoic soul, give away to your emotions...
Smile, laugh and cry out the feelings surging within you...
Pour your heart to hearts that listen, be vulnerable and proud.
Indulge like a child and resist the need to mask.
It's not always about others, you matter most, most of all.
Live your life, be alive, only then does the rest matter.
Flexing muscles and a puffed-up chest are no longer indicators of masculinity.
Age gracefully and with joy, never resist the change.
Follow your passion to the fill, kick the doubts to oblivion.
Men who cry, laugh, share and are vulnerable...
Are the men who shall stand the test of times.
And men who inspire their girls to love.

Words, speak them out..

She grew up hearing heroic tales of Jhansi and Gandhi..
The sweets she ate on Independence Day and the majestic flutter of the flag,
Instilled patriotism in her, the meaning she sought and set forth.
The white robes of Gandhi as he marched in the shores of Dandi,
Symbolised purity in her little mind, the past would reveal, the robes had been soiled.
That purity of mind would have to pay heavy costs, more than one could bear.
The waiting for the Mahatma and Freedom at midnight, evoked the patriot in her.
The blood in her curdled at the atrocities committed, and her heart pained at the lives lost.
Years ahead would reveal that history oft repeated, just the weapons evolved.
Taslima, Khalid and Salman taught her the cost, one would have to bear, on doling out the truth.
Confused was her mind, blood boiled and heart paced, but muted was the voice.
With regret, she oft recollected, how she often opened her mouth to say something.
Blood gushed, but the words failed, if only she had spoken, the world, her world would have been different...
Dejected as she sat, tears welling up in her eyes, the star shone bright, Kalpana she saw, smiling at her.
It's never too late, chimed her heart, and march ahead she did, into the clear blue sky...

In vain

The lady smiled generously at me,
She pulled away her feet and dusted the seat,
So that i could sit, cozy and snug,
I marvelled at her generosity and innocence of her smile.
I thanked the universe for such kind people.
The train chugged along, merrily and in rhythm.
She offered me a sweet, a healthy one,
I politely denied as I was conditioned so,
My heart raced at what i saw next,
She flung the plastic wrapper casually on the tracks.
My wits were numbed and i feigned ignorance at the crime,
I looked away as far as i could, beyond the trees, beneath the waters,
As if i could apologize my helplessness,
But things went from bad to worse,
A little boy was attempting to squeeze, an empty bottle,
Through the reluctant window bars,
And here comes the lady, embodiment of kindness to his rescue,
She took the bottle and flung it afar, beaming with pride.
I sulked and swore, deep in my heart,
Buried under layers of conditioning,
Refrained my soul by speaking thus and hurting mother earth.

The other me

The well-oiled plaits and dim-witted look, the class note book held tight to the bosom.
She walked and sprinted, huffed and puffed, along the paved road to the school.
Gals in dainty dresses and coloured lips, mocked at her 'boring attire'.
The loudspeakers blared and festoons flared, to welcome the hero from the town.
As she looked at the smiling face, that adorned all posters in every nook and corner, spare the drains.
Her heart skipped a beat, and breath grew heavy. Fog covered her sight and lips trembled hard, to still.
The town's hero, they extolled him, garlands of flowers and notes, awaited him.
As the beats grew loud, the heart thudded against her rib cage as if to break it.
Flagrant hair and blazing eyes, she remembered vividly the night before.
Still unable to believe it's her own makeover, she forged ahead with muddled thoughts.
Dancing lights and the drummers' beats had brought out the devil in her.
She danced in fervour till the party left, till the beats waned and the twilight came.
The only one who stood witness with his keen eyes and friendly smile, an amused look at the act.
What transpired had broken to shambles, the mask, society had sculpted over years.
And an uncanny friend in the unchanciest moment, she sought with insanity.

Sinful fun

She toiled day in and out, nursing her forgetful mother,
The mother in her second childhood, but less in frolic,
Clothes were discarded as if least needed,
The garbled speech, reeked of threats and swore of misery,
The girl forgot to smile, as if resigned to her fate,
The youth beset with huge responsibility, no time for cheer,
And up came a lad, who sought her joy,
After, a seemingly mammoth task, of relentless wooing,
He saw a smile, alas a precious treasure,
Small buds of hope erupt in the barren mind of the lass,
She strayed, nay indulged in simple human pleasures,
A song here, a dance there, she tip toed for a glimpse.
And up came, the moralists, brickbats, sticks and stones,
For the huge sin committed in selfish mind,
That self-love she attempted, where sacrifice was the rule.
When the mother ailed, in a lost mind, the daughter shall giveth all,
For nothing is noble as the act of sacrifice, as if the self might care.

A train of thoughts...

Yet another dawn has arisen, no traces of the yester night, good or bad...
As the train chugs along, I struggle to calm my breath and clear my fogged lens...
Another snake glides in the opposite direction, I'm safely embodied in one.
For a moment I think of the estranged souls caught in between tracks...
Oh! What pull would they fall a victim of, as either is fatal...
From the urban to country side as I meander, my mind begins to calm down.
The strains of heavenly music seek to soothe my soul...
I close my eyes in relief, everything is in place...
My kids will be safe, my family will be safe, the virus shall show mercy...
As dawns rays shine on blades of grass, I long to wade naked foot in the paddy.
To lie facing the cosmos in a directionless canoe...
And with no strings attached yet my soul longs for its mate unabashed...
As the dawn gives away to a bold day, my heart longs for the day we shall walk hand in hand...
Our hearts mirroring each other, smiling foolishly...
Oh! For a world sans judgement, where innocence rules...
Hush! Here comes the TTR and with her the harsh reality....

My clothes

The empress has new clothes,
The visible and invisible,
Expensive clothes and perfume,
Flowers and dainty shoes,
A mansion for a lone soul,
A chauffeur driven car,
A swimming pool and an open theatre,
But heavily clothed is the soul, invisibly cloaked,
Apprehensions and insecurity form the fence,
Fear and anger, delude the eyes,
Jealousy and pride form the tiara,
And ego forms the crown,
I hope a day shall arise,
When ye realise, the futility of thy cloaks
Both visible and invisible,
For ye were born naked and so shall thee leave,
Better realise now or never,
For a realised moment shall be a treasure,
Treasure to the naked, beautiful soul.

For a tomorrow that shall never come

When my heart throbbed, imploring me to speak out my love...
I held myself back for a morrow...
When I wished I could forgive him, my vengeance chimed.
Not yet, let tomorrow come...
When my heart voiced it's love for travel,
The pragmatic me refrained, saying it's not the time...
When my heart pranced about with my kids...
My mind said, your joints are weak, let's wait for tomorrow.
When I wished to tell sorry and get away even, my ego halted me.
You needn't bow down today, tomorrow shall come.
When I wished to sit still bathed in moonlight and embraced by love.
My mind chided, you have better things to do, get going.
My untold love, unforgiven scars and hidden desires live on...
In the enigma for a tomorrow that shall never come...
The objects of my passion shall wither and fade, but the stoic ego still waits.
In enigma for a tomorrow that shall never come...
Worthless the wait for tomorrow that shall never come.

Bokeh, the blur

The days began with the search for truth...
Something finite would dole out for sure...
The bards sang, the scriptures spelt...
The lines were drawn, who did what, who was what...
Wrongs were punished and rights were applauded...
Thus when the sun rose and set as predicted...
When status and honour were the only priority...
Somewhere, the leaves rustled, showing a path hitherto unknown...
A seeker went in search of truth, the 'ultimate truth'.
Soon the lines began to blur, shades of grey popped in.
Love and lust, rich and poor, sin and sinner, right and wrong...
The dictates no longer held fast, the chains loosened itself...
Cries of passion, either in joy, sorrow or fear reached muffled to the ears...
The truth seemed near, the weariness wore off...
But what lays ahead, when the truth is known...
Another line waiting to be blurred...the Bokeh effect...

It is ok

It is ok to not speak, the anguish in your heart,
If all the audience are a judging lot.
It is ok to hide your deepest desires,
Lest the people around are a mocker lot.
It is ok to not express your love always,
When your soul is tired, weary and all.
It is ok to not prove your point,
Coz people have perspective diverse as they are.
It is ok if someone hurt you,
To get hurt or not is your choice.
It is ok to express your love,
The thing of beauty won't last forever.
It is ok to indulge in the desires of your soul,
It is your desire and your soul after all.
It is ok to say no, whenever you want,
You are your own decision maker.
It's ok if your friend or lover rejects you,
You are your best friend and lover.
It's ok to go against the rule book,
For no one told it's the ultimate truth.
The right and the wrong are your own doing,
Follow your heart, it's ok o! Pal.

The bud of hope

For a long time, I believed that religious bigotry got the upper hand,
That blind baseless beliefs had found roots in so-called educated minds,
That the silence of the people to atrocities was deafening,
Yet now the bud has blossomed, the bud of hope into the secular flower,
For years I believed that the writers of truth had disapparated,
Vanquished or relinquished, it remained to decipher,
Vague plots and shallow writing were extolled for the safe talk,
Freedom of expression no longer existed,
And one had to express in unheard whispers,
Very far from the ideals of the constitution of our Country,
Yet again, the bud has blossomed, the bud of hope into the expressive flower.

Ego

For days, i fought, my enemies, their words,
The battlefield that glistened with blood, adding to guilt and remorse.
It seemed a vicious circle, the foes and the plots,
I couldn't see the horizon, nay a flicker of hope,
The enemy seemed to be a dementor, hollowing out my essence,
I whined, got whipped, whined again, exhausted I was no doubt.
Then sometime when my sword lay low, I wondered where the foe hid,
In awe I realise it was my ego, inflated, threatening to burst, any time.
No, it didn't burst, but fizzled out, as I let go, wearily,
I realise, I need never put up a fight, coz there was none, for the sword,
And the sword, it was pure fiction, of my ego ridden mind,
The sparks do fly, the threats loom large, yet I'm at peace, o! Pal,
I realise, I have nothing to lose, for nothing was there to lose,
And for me, I existed, in oblivion of the miniscule being I was,
And now I let go, of you and me, but I find greater love and peace,
The death has begun with the birth of love.

Born wrong, but now refined

She had tresses that coiled a little too much,
Smoothening just made it right.
The skin was a bit too dark, a touch up would set things right,
She smiled a bit too much, a snigger would do just right,
The pitch was a bit too high, hushing up would set the tone,
Paddy fields and star lit skies lit up her face,
But she sought happiness amidst the concrete jungle.
So many she wooed, but yet fell short,
Too tall, too short, too dark, too smart,
So many 'toos' failed her chances.
Little did she know the gem she was,
Raw and unchiselled and chosen to shine.
Little did she know the might within,
Masked by feeble minds that surrounded her.

Fuming embers…

The ancient doors creaked open, the aura held so strong...
A fragrance so sweet and intense, lingered in my senses..
Of wretched souls and blood stained orbs, the dreams were one and all..
The passion and the warm glow, lit the hollow ablaze.
After weary trails and fruitless struggles with ego and the guilt,
I looked forth in the canopy for the clearing that would come...
I refuse to be a smooth pebble chiselled by the rough water...
Through naysayers and sooth sayers, I seek a middle path...
A challenge I await, in my wake, sharpening the edge of my sword...
So, when the bell does toll, the strike shall fall sure and hard...

Chillax

There's nowhere to go, nothing to do and no one to please, o! Pal,
For the targets, goals and objectives are not the ultimate ones,
Heave a sigh, take a halt and gulp a breath of air,
They weigh mighty and high in the balance of life,
The dress you choose, the gait of yours and the words you speak, my pal...
Let them flow liberal and true, true to thy self, o ! Soul.
The ones you love, embrace them tight,
The wrongs you suffered, forgive and let go,
The childhood dreams and the buried passions,
Let them live and chase them to the core.
Visit, the long-forgotten pals, and the once cherished haunts,
Let them see the new vibrant you, the real you.

The warmth of life

Tears trickled down my eyes and sweat from my brow.
Never was breathing so laborious.
Shallow breather that I was, catching a breath seemed so precious.
The mask thrust on my face, infused life air into tired lungs.
I looked bleary eyed, at my comrades in distress.
Little could I do to help, either me or them,
White dementors nay angels, roamed the place trying to take or give spirit.
I remembered how once I too had been in the cast, aloof albeit helpless.
Happy memories of the yore floated before my eyes.
Strains of haunting music caught my ears.
Just as I sank blissfully into the bottomless abyss, light as a feather,
I felt a grasp, a warm blooded one and a gasp, a wisp of warm breath.
I looked aghast nay amazed at the deep-set eyes, kind yet firm,
Firm in the resolve to yank me back, into the world of reality.
It's not yet time, the voice did chime, and lingered on in my heart.
And slowly and surely the amasked and agloved angel, prodded me back to life...
Life that was full, teeming with colour and buzzing with gay spirit.

The elephant again

As is conceived, sometimes man is blinded,
By an intelligence, unique to oneself, equated to ego,
As he is groping in the dark, with his fellow comrades,
The oft narrated story unfolds, of the umpteen shapes of the elephant,
Here, the elephant, a person, a situation or an opinion in vogue,
But no consensus is reached despite the pool of intelligence,
The quagmire of opinions and the fights that ensue,
What then is difference between a blind one and thee?
Well, for a respite! the elephant ran amok, blinded by the blind.

Unlearning

As years pass, here I stand, my cup empty and thirsty...
I poured away all that didn't appeal to my soul...
I learn it is easy and normal to love seamlessly..
It's ok to shout when you are met with injustice.
It's ok to laugh out loud when your soul is tickled,
Being a child and reliving childhood fantasies is perfectly normal..
There is no need to pump up your chest, exhale with all might...
Dark circles and flab are perfectly normal..
Sexuality is as normal a need as air and water..
No longer is it needed to smile when your soul cries..
Feeling and expressing emotions are and were always normal...
No one tells you not to follow your heart, your inner voice, but you...
Children are masters of spirituality, follow them no doubt..
How you look, speak and think are purely your decision...
Your ultimate lover unto the end is you and you alone..
And I'm grateful for the wonderful gift that I am in the making..
Gathering the pearls, I move forward, looking to gather more...

Me

Beyond this body, beyond these thoughts,
I exist wholesome and at peace,
Beyond these expectations and these experiences,
I exist serene and sans expectations,
Beyond this passion and the lust,
I exist, a reservoir of love, endless,
Beyond the sighs and the tears,
I exist in utter silence, ever so still,
Beyond these pangs and loneliness,
I exist in childlike joy,
Of myriad experiences is my life replete,
To whisper of the treasures within,
I skim, I swim and dive within,
Lost in me, in blissful mirth.

Home

It is a place where iam born into feeble and hapless...
When survival is my soul motto, food, water and cuddles,
my tools for survival..
Slowly patterns emerge, and I'm pulled into the crux...
Neither of free will or liking, the cyclone revolves...
In the continuous revolutions, I fall dizzy headed,
yielding to come what may...
Occasionally when the sky is clear, I observe threads of
reality, of a world outside...
A home outside, in the streets, in another soul, within my
body...
Thoughts once alien, but now worth exploring...
Travel and people delight me, so do books and lone
beaches...
New homes I discover, more appealing to the self, my
self...
Letting go is neither bad nor so scary, and free will comes
to me...
I discover my will to choose, my new homes, endearing to
my soul.
Slowly and surely, I expand my wings and soar, to
discover new homes,
In thither lands, where my spirit shall laugh unabashed and
savour the blossoms of joy.

Unwritten

The pen shivers, at the enormity of thoughts,
It's like an earthquake, come to life,
What if they were written, for eyes to read,
Maybe an explosion would ensue, no doubt,
Maybe a string of 'em, in nooks and corners,
Hitherto concealed, as is true about truth,
The urge is strong to pen 'em all, yet it wilts,
The might, wheedled by sanity, so far from reality,
Hence I chose to conceal, and let loose a string of masks,
Masks that hide the word, taint it and paint it,
Making it impotent and maimed,
For that's what the world loves,
To see and believe all is well, in the fool's world.

Relish

It is like the feel of tender dew covered grass on parched
and bruised feet..
It is like the feel of cool, moisture laden air on hot,
perspiring skin...
It is the joy laden golden ray, that sneaked into a dungeon
of despair...
It is the smile and the rolling tears, when seeing your
beloved after ages...
It is the secret hope that fills your heart when the whip
misses your chance...
It is the wide smile on the toddler's face, when embraced
by her mom...
It is the feeling of cool water awash your dry throat as you
gulp down in thirst...
It is the negative result of an unpleasant test, to show you
are free from the virus...
It is the anticipation that builds in the heart of lovers
before they finally meet...
It is being pampered by funky blankets as you go burying
yourself deeper and deeper...
It is the fragrance of earth getting wet under the drizzle of
summer rains...

Into the fire

I was drawn to you, like life to death,
Or a greater life, fatal attraction.
Singeing my wings, the nearer i came,
Your glow cast a spell, a deathly one, it was.
My mind flitted furiously, in vain,
Trying to beat sense into a clouded mind.
Yet my heart drew me closer, to the glorious danger.
Somehow, i felt, so certain, in tooth and nail.
There was nothing to lose, nowhere to go.
And here i go, bereft of wings, bereft of senses,
Drifting slow but sure, into fathomless abyss.
My body still as a rock, yet my mind in eternal bliss.
I owe you, O fire!, a life sans rebirth.

The bell does ring

Deep down in the depths of my heart,
Dwells a spirit, covered in snow and cold,
But every year as Christmas arrives,
It shakes it off, the snow and doubt,
From within, the warmth, melts away the ice,
That mars the magical spirit,
And here i go, in the skies, clutching my sleigh.
The bell does ring, loud and melodious, echoing in my ears,
My heart is filled with a warmth and joy, the year unto end,
I laugh and prance, mad with joy, eyes ever sparkling,
For Christmas is here, my love, to stay, for the spell is true.
I believe as never before, the magic in my life,
The wisps of doubt fade away, in the might of love.
Miracles abound and delight me abound,
I realise again and again, sometimes the most real things,
In the world are things we can't see.

A knock on the head

She draped herself in 3 yards of cotton,
Slowly adeptly, checking the pleats,
Her ear was keen on counting the whistles of her cooker,
Her mind raced, checking the inaginary to do list,
The vermillion red on the forehead,
The mangalsutra to prove her chastity,
Sometimes she wondered the need, yet complied,
For she was a dutiful wife, doting to the end.
Clothes strewn over, dishes heaped in the sink,
All were her hearts calling, for they proved her mettle,
The superwoman that she was, storming the house, a human robot.
The husband's endearing words and gestures of affection were rewards,
For the sacrifice of her time, tidiness of the house, tidiness of the kids,
Her body needed little food, little pleasure and hard work,
Mottos for a successful life, and so the internet baba says.
Somewhere along she met a soul, who took her senses to ridicule.
She was mocked at and ridiculed for the effort put in.
Somewhere she saw a light blink, sending rays of realisation.
She knows now how precious is her body alias home.
She looked deep into her eyes, and saw the inner child pleading for justice.
And now she walks, no longer sprints,
No longer super, but a lot sane,
One with aches and pains, but tolerant of it all.
The sense of justice so profound, yet so silent of it all.
The journey has just begun, yet unfaltering in her stride.

Iam because we are

On knowing that you and i are the same in and out,
That the essence is the same before the form,
That your form and beliefs are just an egoic shadow,
Of the formless, beautiful essence that resides in you,
I see me in you, and all the beings, alive and not,
I see me in the plants,trees, animals and birds,
And i know how it feels to be choked with plastic,
I realise how painful words can be, I'm careful with them,
I forgive the unconscious for the mindless blabber,
I know that I needn't be the vehicle of anyone's beliefs or egos,
I realise the spirit of true freedom, and the value of kindness,
I know that more layers remain to be unravelled,
I wish the schools taught the true meaning of love and freedom,
Sans conditions San beliefs, that the little ones are the true teachers,
Of the adults to be, of the mankind in evolution,
Let them be, nurture them as they are, never manipulate,
See them in you and you in them, see you in all that is around you,
I'm sure you shall then live a kinder life, full of love and gratitude sans expectation.

The half baked adult

I disliked my friend for the way she took care of her pencils,
Why should she behave so perfectly, so like an adult?
I disliked the other for the marks she scored,
And another for her pretty looks, and diligence,
I disliked him for his oratory skills, leaving me helpless,
Scrambling for words, never able to express my thoughts,
I lived in a world where hugs, cuddles and kisses were exclusive,
For the smart, diligent and capable kids,
I for one was clumsy, careless, lazy to the core,
A massive project for improvement, the progress, dismal,
Love was purely conditional, and needed to be fought for,
Never given freely to the lazy and clumsy kids out there,
You had to earn love, by hardwork, by rising early and score high.
Looks were always average, never worth a mention,
I felt safe in larger than size outfits i wore and behind my spectacles,
Somehow i believed i would always remain a child under shelter,
Adulthood was not for me, O! How terrifying it was,
But now here iam, an adult yet to be free,
From the invisible knots of sour childhood memories.

Chores that heal

Sometimes as the world around you is in a whirl,
A kingdom of chaos all around, the mind in a senseless labyrinth,
I seek refuge in the household chores, once abhorred by me,
Just a rhythmic scrubbing, washing away the dirt,
Putting them away, sparkling and clean,
Attempts to cleanse the rot, that tries to engulf my mind,
The mundane task of laundry that i oft accuse of stripping me,
Of my creativity and free time, and time with the kids,
Is now a life saver, as I drowned amongst the sea of clothes,
Folding, sorting and stocking, it does the trick, no doubt.
As i wipe the dust off counters and engage,
In all such miniscule tasks, that devour my time,
I'm left feeling grateful for the ingenious way,they saved me,
From the clasp of thoughts, thoughts that weren't up to any good.
Things have come to a point, that as the chaos emerge, I'm left to fend for chores,
Chores that slowly bring me back to the world, to ground me.

I have a back, be still

Yes, i have a back, as often reminded,
By the acute stabs that accompany leaning,
I never thought how precious it was, until,
The twists and turns and every posture was laden with pain,
Oh!, The throes of pain, different from yester years,
As now I relate to it and a moment to grow spiritually,
A lesson learnt the hard way, to let go, always,
People are going about their own business, or in search,
Of a greater purpose in life, either way,
I have no need to interfere, let them go,
Time to pause and reflect, coz that's all that can be done,
Pain-free and still, reckoning to the present to reveal,
More of its treasures, each a lesson,
Well learnt the hard way, nailed to the core...
Rest O! Soul, coz you have a back, be still,
As it hurts as embers, seething and fuming.
Yet stillness is healing for the mind and body, be still.

Co passengers

The train chugged along, rhythmically and noisily,
The ripples slowly moved afar from the source of origin,
The capped man, swiped his phone, engrossed in visual display,
Blue light gleamed on the cheeks of the man at work in his laptop,
The lady who was incessantly chattering about the burdens of her life,
Was now irrevocably silent, as if held in a trance,
So individual, so different, yet bound together in ways unseen,
We travelled, passengers of the shatabdi,
Some toddler cried, trying vainly to resist the clutches of her mom,
The clutches of safety, oh, how long will they last, sometimes, a lifetime.
“Water, water!”, the man cried, as if to quench the insatiable thirst,
The thirst of the soul, or the hunger, growing by the minute,
The drama unfolds, of umpteen expressions,
Beyond the navarasas, diverse is mankind in ways unseen.
As it is time to descend, i bid farewell, to my co passengers,
A silent prayer that kindness and peace prevails in their life,
That we are all together no matter what.

The human baby

It was born feeble and helpless,
Unable to stand erect and run until a year,
And when it did stand and run,
Slowly fears filled the ears and mind.
Clouding the brilliance it was born with.
Unlike the brothers in the forest who lived in the present,
It fretted about the past and the unknown future,
Though evidence lay in annals of history,
Of its herculean might and indefatigable spirit,
Of mind boggling creations and stupendous feats,
Yet it chose to discard the truths with a disdain, well trained.
The falls whether physical or mental,
Were feared more than the actual fall.
Little did it know, or yet believe,
The wise words of Rumi,
That the wound is the place where the light enters you.

Who am I?

I'm your little secret, so beautifully hidden,
I'm the bud that blossoms in the midst of the night,
I'm the flower that brims with nectar,
And spreads fragrance to but, one,
I'm the incense that ceases to burn as the dawn arrives,
My desires I hide, behind cloaks, so thick,
Sometimes even smothered to naught,
Who sees them, or hears of them,
I know not, yet despair, that some day shall come,
When I cease to be but a secret, but a flower that blooms in dawn,
That my tears flow to wash out, years of trepidation.
That I breathe free, naked and pure...

Hijacked

Sometimes the fear is beyond words,
The wide, abysmal chasms,
The tight rope walks above the canyons,
Life in a destitute home, alone and in misery,
Lurking fears in dark jungles,
Eerie sounds in dark corridors,
Departure from the dearest ones,
The roaring of the deep, feary sea in storm,
Umpteen are the fantasies that creep,
And slowly hijack my brain,
Fearful am I to go to sleep,
The calm reassurance of the croaking frogs,
The rhythmic hum of the cicadas, music to my ears,
I fear the world that waits to unfold,
Once my eyes are closed and I drift off to sleep,
The dreamworld is one of scares, much unlike the real world.

My car

I sat in you decked as a bride, tear stained cheeks and clouded mind.
Slowly and slowly your elegance captured my eyes,
Stoic yet savvy, sleek yet chunky.
I fell in love with you, our journeys together.
A home you were, cozy to the core.
Unfailing friend through the kilometres traversed,
Strange roads and uninhabited lands,
We crossed many a mile, you with me,
I prayed for you, to escape theft, rampant in the area.
I nursed my baby in your cosy folds, she mewled and puked.
I love every bit of you, you are my home, my ever sojourn,
Somewhere along the journey of life,
Our lives entwined inseparably,
Guess you were send, so I could have the safest travels ever.
I trusted you with my family and you stood grounded, my pal.
And here now as we part ways, a sigh escapes my heart.
I wish you peaceful days with the new family you are in.
Encore, my pal your flawless performance and steal their hearts for good.

Home of yonder

I miss my home of yonder,
Where laughs echoed in the corridors,
Where smells from the kitchen, flooded my senses,
Where the shouts and cries of cousins in mirth,
Filled the air, with delight.
Where the paw marks of Jimmy were all over the place,
Where make believe ghosts and eerie sounds,
Send chills along the spine of toddlers
Where crows crowed perched on the thatched roof,
Where the rooster chased us with its blood curdling cry,
The hushed nights spend huddled in seeing horror movies,
The delightful powercuts prowling in the dark,
Oh, I wish I were a child again, chasing the shadows,
Of fond memories, long gone

Rain

As a child, dark clouds made me gloomy as the sun was out of sight,
So were, the play ground and my friends,
Yet as it rained with all the drama,
Something lightened in my heart,
A feeling that came back with every rain,
I sniffed and inhaled, the smell of wet earth,
The moist breeze caressing my cheeks,
It awakened feelings of desire, I blushed,
As paper boats sailed in streams, eventually meeting,
The fate of the unsinkable,
As drops made puddles and rivulets,
I watched wonderstruck at the beauty of it all,
The evening lamp, the kajal lined eyes,
The swaying mango leaves and the mystic serpent grove,
All struck a poignant note, in the harp of my soul,
I pined for you, as the hornbill for rain,
Beyond the sheets of water, beneath the pregnant mango tree,
I see you standing, in folded arms,
For a moment I wait for the rain to ebb off,
But who was I fooling, for you and the rain,
Are inseparable and one, Oh! quencher of thirst,
Of the mind and body, and thus I drench myself to the core,
Till the bliss engulfs me beyond words…

I wish upon

I wish upon the wave of a wand,
To take me away to places of lure,
Where the sun casts sparkles over timid waves,
Where the moonlight lights up the valley in ethereal beauty,
Where kids frolic in mirth and glee,
Least mindful of the worries of adult hood,
Where toadstools line the magic ring,
The fairy ring of Blyton lore,
Where delicious soups and breathtaking aromas,
Fill the senses with umami, to the body and mind,
Where the canoe glides smooth over tranquil waters,
And kites colour the sapphire blue sky,
Where kindred souls gather in silence around a fire,
Their hearts brimming with a love so rare,
Where verdant green are the country sides,
Dainty, pretty houses echoing with soulful laughter,
Magic hovering and filling every nook and corner

My moon

When you smiled at me, coyly and in cool delight,
I longed to gaze at you in the coziness of my room,
And then i saw you from my window smiling in my room,
A star twinkled near you, your friend, one apart from me,
The silhouetted leaves of the coconut tree, played hide and seek with you,
You send me the cool breeze that caressed my skin as always,
And i sensed your query, of what took me so long,
So long since we met, the last time when i was sixteen,
My hearts troubles i poured to you,
You heard them out, patient and consistent,
And never once did you wince, or play hide and seek,
And never failed to heal me with your tender, cool touch,
Mortals may die, but you remain and eternal friend,
A tender witness to the non physical realm, where my cherished ones rest.

The glow

It was dark, pitch black, a velvety night.
The air teemed with croaks and incessant chirping of crickets,
The downpour had just ceased,
A Cool breeze wafts through the curtains, luring me…
To the feast that awaited, amidst the dark.
It was as if the stars dropped down, some comets too…
So enchanting and magical, i watched spellbound.
The gigantic silhouettes of trees swayed gently, rocked by the wind.
A calm descended, a blanket of peace.
Hushing the numerous thoughts that arose,
For it is time to savour the present, and savour i shall, i swear.

Whisper of the woods

The trail was long and strewn with leaves...
The whispers of the woods reached my ears...
An eerie stillness filled the air...and a heaviness engulfed me...
For a moment I feared the loneliness..
But the kind eyes of the sambar deer eased the anguish...
The deer sprinted crushing the leaves in its trail..
Leaving me alone to explore the truths the woods spelt...
Far from the madding crowd, far from the entangled thoughts...
I realised the blurring of lines between the right and wrong...
How easy it was to love and how difficult to hate..
The cicadas and crickets competed in the concert..
Leaving the onlookers no wiser than before..
The woody smells and champa flowers filled ones lung with glee..
As I walk beneath towering trees, I realise how insignificant I am..
So my thoughts and my dreams are mine alone to savour..
Farewell dear friend, a day shall come, when I shall be back..
As a breeze I shall blow into you and rustle your leaves in mirth..

Timeless love

As I looked on, the silhouettes had merged...into the ink black sky...
A cool breeze ushered in the fragrance of pala blossoms...
Somewhere in the vicinity, I wonder if I heard sighs...
Nimble fingers, that worked through ebony tresses...
A lass who bore a forlorn look, in her sad beautiful eyes...
To be or not to be, to love or not to love, she struggled in the knots...
Slowly the glitters were spilt over the night sky...
The stars shone like never before, as if to light her path...
The moon smiled at the innocent queries that escaped from her silence..
The cosmos whispered in her ears, go on.. O! Lass..go on..
Halt the wait and venture forth, for that's the way to tread....
For love, O! Lass, hath no age and hath no wrongs soever...
And love is to be given, never to be hidden, for the soul shall fume in the loss..

Evening hues

The coconut leaves tried to marr the glory of the sun,
It was as if knives were chiseling at the Kohinoor,
Moringa leaves swayed ever so gently, like bells on a jhumka,
And the jackfruit tree moved in it's majestic stance,
It was a pleasure to watch the dusk set in,
Pigeons crooned and crows cawed ushering the loved ones,
Back to the nest, for it was time for love and rest,
I sat in my terrace lost in the sights unfolding before my eyes,
How trivial human worries seemed to the omnipresent peace,
For all this fretful chatter comes to naught,
When the bell does toll, and it's time to leave,
All that remains is a bouquet of memories of times good and bad,
But yet the breeze shall blow and waves come forth...

Water

It flowed, brimming as a brook, gathering fallen leaves,
Chiselling pebbles to perfection, making way through tenuous rocks,
Thrusting, nurturing, surrendering and erasing,
Slowly building up in the lovers eye, salted with longing, of love,
Drizzling on leaves, washing away the dirt, leaving em' free to breathe,
The uneasy calm of the lake, teeming with life down beneath,
Overwhelming waves that swallow mankind, bereft of explanation,
As if a cleansing is all that's required, the Noah's ark, nowhere in sight.
Where one prays for a drop to quench, the parched earth,
The other prays just as fervently to quell the mighty tides of fury,
For all one might know, the vastness of its motherly love,
As it plays with the wiggling toes of the delightful toddler,
So oblivious of the vicissitudes of mother water...

The trees

It is happy, where it is,
It is thriving, slow but strong,
Let it be happy where it is,
Let it grow, sure and big,
Let it expand and dream great dreams,
Let the branches touch the sky,
Let it grow into the beautiful tree, it is destined to be,
You, my friend are another tree,
Your branches may intertwine,
The wind may take your leaves there,
The wind may whistle and whisper in both your ears,
You may wish, for the wind, a messenger of love,
Yet know that though your branches meet,
You are worlds apart,
Your roots run in different worlds,
You may wither and wilt in different times,
Don't be carried away by the wind,
Stay rooted at all times my dear.

Bespectacled dreams…

Those days when the endoderm and the ectoderm of the cotyledon seemed to merge ....
The frequent misspelt words, the red circles and wrongs...
My science teacher sought a reason beyond my numbed looks...
Then began my world, behind the large spectacles, from 7 years of inception ...
Almirahs seemed to bulge and bullies extra rude, when behind the lens..
Once I abhored, then I felt low and slowly it became my companion for life...
For the dew drops, the tender buds and the beauty of the dawn...
Seemed more beautiful and real behind the lens..
The blur53 of the world without my friend has given me the shivers many a day...
So I clasp tight the legs and fit them hard to home, lest they fall off.. blinding me...
Many a year had passed and so did my collection of 'em in various shapes and sizes...grow..
One special friend I cherished lies today buried by sand under the waters of Hoganakkal...
A little fidgety, a little unsure and a little introvert I remain...
As my world is complete only with you my friend...
But together we have miles to go, stay close and leave me not when the plunge I take...

The voice within

It all began in the years of the plaits..
Hundreds of voices advised me ever..
Torn between indecision and frustration I plodded down my path..
With envy I oft looked at the diligent trail of ants..
The plethora of emotions seemed non existent in them..
Not one decision, ever pleased the cosmos cause diversity reined the helm..
And fear of wrongdoing, kept me knotted in my knees..
Oft many a soul came along, veiled with empathy...
Dim witted, I fell often, to the honey cladded words...
And when the soul doth awake, the vails were loud and deep in the vacuum...
And hate wound, it's stealthy coils around the trunk of guilt..
From the black hole, when I emerge, the soft voice whispers loud..
Trust not, but thy intuition, and the chime of your heart...
For when the soul is light and warm, the path treaded is right..
And in thy path, the soft breeze shall whisk away the doubts..
And fears that the doubts bringeth shall no longer hold strong...

The gift of today

The little eyes looked on at the tadpoles in play ....
The fish in a riot of colours gave away to giggles in gay..
Rounded pebbles and crystal waters cleared the fear in her...
Life is so simple, flow in the present, the past is gone forever.
Though the diagnosis spelt doom, the smile of the doctor...
Was enough to kindle her spirit, and the hope fairy did wave..
Her magic wand once and for all, the fear took flight never to alight ever again...
And the little girl held out her hand, for the drizzle to drench her fate..
So that she could hide her tears in the torrents of downpour...
For tonight is the only night she shall cry over the past...

Swim away, Oh! Thoughts!!

Hundreds of fish swim in my mind..
Some bright and luminescent..
Some pale and innocuous...
The bright ones tweak the corners of my mouth into a loud great smile...
The pale ones tense my mind into a tight walking rope..
The paleness an enigma, instills a fear in me..
A fear of the unknown, the seeking of colours, the eerie stillness..
A melody gives away to cacophony and an abrupt end...
The need to break away from the oft mundane life...
Never bequeath your dreams to the abyss awaiting ahead..
The whirlpool shall not pull in the strings of hope, rather it should evert a volcano..
The fragrant lava that blazes to ashes all who doubt indefinitely..
And go forth the soul shall, eyes open, the fishes swimming away in the torrents..

Ecstasy

The tiara glittered and the bangles clinked..
As she twirled around, the mirrors on her skirt, shone like a thousand suns..
The myrrh wafted deep into the nostrils, uninvited in some...
With half closed eyes and graceful moves, she swayed with the beats..
The coloured beads on her full bosom shimmering in the light..
Just like the riot of colours that she displayed..
A riot of conflicting thoughts engulfed the onlookers..
Oblivious to the havoc, she swayed in vibrant moves...
The graceful curves and flawless looks embodied a gem..
A silent thread she spun around entwining all the souls...
For right or wrong nothing mattered in the spur of the moment..
An ecstasy it wrought so deep, in the hearts of her audience..
Nods and claps and tapping toes, accompanied the addictive beats...
At the end of the charm when the trance did break, the lone sane one smiled in enigma...

The other side

The windows were open, as usual this sunny morning..
The sun's rays glided stealthily into the room, oh how lucky the sun was..
All I could do was stand here and guess the beauty of her face in the golden glow..
Sweet was the fragrance that I whiffed eagerly, everytime the windows opened..
Pretty were the hands that pushed the windows..
And lustrous were her locks, from a lucky glimpse or two..
Day and night I chose to linger in my yard, yearning for a glimpse of the pearl, in her oyster...
Within the room, things were a shade of gloom..
Envy she did, the lad in the yard, lucky was he to see the sun..
To hear the whistle of the birds and bask in the warmth..
To let the wind rustle his dishevelled crown..
She lay in wait, for the day, when her wounds would heal..
When she could face the world, scars and all..
She wondered at the ephemeral love that wafted in the air..
The transcience of it all, made her laugh, a deep hollow laugh .

Soul talk

Jittery as i sat, an examiner, restless in my seat,
Then came the students, steady in a spree.
At once i noticed, the windows to their souls.
So clear, sparkling and innocent,
The souls within beckoned to me.
Some pleaded with their eyes, some hid mischief.
Some shone with happiness, yet others looked afar, beyond me.
Though it was a span of 2 minutes, yet i wished it would last longer.
It was a new hobby, this one, of looking into thine eyes.
One couldn't hide, behind the mask,
Or distractions like the nose, the beard.
The eyes were all, the only windows for a heartful talk.
So, here i go talking with my eyes too, being as kind as i could be.
For, it was a soul to soul talk, unmasked and bare to the core.

Into the ocean

As she wound herself in the last few yards of her new sari,
She observed the mutinous feelings creeping within her mind.
Proud of her curves and unsurpassed beauty, she looked on...
Somewhere feelings of envy and fear gripped her in hiding.
Unable to decipher the source, she tried to restore the grin or grimace...
So sought after by the camaraderie.
Weary yet unable to retire, she pulled forward haltingly.
Would anyone conspire that a iconic beauty of her stature,
Could be fighting a battle of identity within herself.
Things had come to a pass, a do or die situation, the hour foretold.
As she packed her belongings, in the minimalist manner possible.
Mindful, minimal and grateful, she slowly vacated her niche.
Detached and free, yet peaceful and ecstatic, the steps increased in pace.
Oblivious to the chaos that would arise in her absence,
She walked, nay ran away and out into the ocean that awaited her, once and for all.

The boring one

A lass so boring, her words a whisper.
The gait not feline, nor nay a damsel,
Friends a handful, but rock solid.
The beauties chimed in a chorus,
"Oh, how boring she can be?"
Pity her looks and her ways...
God alone knows, what lay in store for her?!
Beneath the misty lens and the dull facade,
Lay a world of dreams, vivid in colours.
The beauty within, she chose to be mum.
How would anyone believe her, the boring one?
She lived in a world of her own,
A world where she flew far and wide...
Her wings stretched out, the wind in her hair...
She longed to set the bird free, so desperate,
The thread weaved itself into visions,
Waiting to unfold into miracles, so sought after.
Desire and passion are not falsehood, O, Pal!
Wait and watch, till you gape, in wonder.
She chuckled, the next time, she heard the word, 'boring'.

I miss my paati

Once i sought solace in her warm lap,
I loved to see her smug smile, following my hug.
I loved listening to her tales of snakes and ghosts, uncanny ones,
Of her tales of valour, the valiant Unniarcha, protector of her family,
From all things, wild and supernatural,
Snakes, rats, ghosts and the likes...
I loved her rasams, unni appams and delicacies,
I loved her beautiful laughing face,
Red, betel stained teeth, and laughing eyes,
The glittering nose ring and her sindoor, later replaced by sober ash.
I miss how i hid behind her back to escape the cane of my dad,
How fiercely she protected me from the spankings in queue.
I miss her age old superstitions, and her myths,
Of demigods, i still strain my ears to hear at night,
I miss her scowls and frowns when i playfully foil her rules,
As now she moves with the aid of her walker,
Lonely and frail, counting her days,
Losing her memory, sight and hearing,
And with it, a treasure trove of stories, hitherto unknown,
Lying concealed beneath, time and lost memory,
I look deep into her eyes, trying to discern my long lost grandmother,
To her again, her tales of valour, my dear own paati...

My boy

The night has fallen, it's time to cuddle,
As you wrap your little arms around me, i feel blessed,
Your dimpled cheeks and toothless smile, i shall cherish in my memories,
The warmth of your little body and your heart thumping against mine,
I wish these times were endless my love,
The cute innocence that emanates from you, dispels all fears to oblivion,
As you cover me with your kisses and love, unseen tears wet my cheeks,
I wish for you, that all your dreams come true my boy,
And that you always remain aware of the love in you and others,
That you grow up to be a man who loves himself and his brethren,
And one who respects and loves his sisters and all life around,
That you continue to wonder at the beauty of dew drops and gurgling streams,
You are always loved, my darling, no matter what.

To my music teacher, with love

Oh, sire, thou art some where in this world,
I choose to believe, happy and at peace,
Singing songs, soulful ones,
The songs you taught, I ever so remember,
A sigh from the depths of my heart,
Patriotism, romance, joy and what not,
U gave us a jig and a magic wand,
The spell holds true, to this day.
My kids sing your songs, etched into eternity,
The joy they bring, the echoes of the choir,
The feeling defies all words,
The punch in my tummy and pull at my nose,
So memorable as if yesterday,
The tears that sprang as patriotism,
Raged in our veins,
The light of love that filled our chests,
As we sang songs of love, true love,
No words, dear sire, I bow in reverence,
Gratitude for the soulful music, you opened the door to.

My teachers

From a great critic like you, I learn,
How not to be so impassionate,
As I empathise with the receiver,
From the uncanny silence, you espouse,
I realise how it is to be a listener,
From the absence of your support,
I learning to stand on two feet,
From your incessant judgements,
I learn to be non-judgemental,
From your varied bitter reactions,
I learn to respond in kindness,
From the absence of a kind ear,
I retreat to the kindness in me,
From unmet expectations,
I learn to suffice for myself,
From unheard lamentations,
I learn to tap into solace within.
To my umpteen teachers,
I owe my heartfelt gratitude,
I have learnt the extent of power,
That lay dormant within me.

The trail…

The multicolored flag fluttered in the breeze..
Lanterns swayed in the cool breeze..
Shadows lengthened on the cobblestone walkway..
A sigh slipped my lips, weary were my eyes, burdened were my shoulders..
Rest, I sought with an eager body..
But the soul within flamed in glee..the tongues engulfed the weariness..
A hot bowl of soup and a hot water bath seemed so tempting to the core..
As always, I assured the child within, the last lap is the hardest..
The trail would soon end and so would my journey..
The twinkling stars and serene moon would let me vent my agony..
They who know all, but remain silent cause some secrets are meant to be..
At last the trail ends, I knock hard..
The smell of hot soup and fragrance of flowers..the tender touch..
Arouse me to the core, and arise I did from the fathoms, from my deep slumber..
Tonight is a night of sorts, a night for quaint noble souls..a night of liberty..

A soul in flames…

The fire was up and burning, the crackling loud to the ears...
The bhansuri played it’s music, plaintive thoughts lingered...
The souls that gathered had little in common sans the cause they gathered for...
Yet some invisible thread of hope bonded them in joy..
The sparks in the firewood and the gleaming embers melted the stony hearts..
The warmth that spread vanished the cold and lit a light within..
Trembling lips and misty eyes spelt the truth within..
Above the stars in the velvety sky shone with a sparkle never seen...
And below the moon shimmered in the still crystal waters...
And deep within the chambers echoed, in the music loud and sweet...
For one moment, in eternity, I felt one with the cosmos, the spell never shalt break...

Anew

The buzz of the city life had stretched my nerves taut...
Too many expectations and too little time paced up my heart...
Grey hairs popped and crow legs too but heck I was busy...
Weary times had only respite in smiles of my besties...
Many a time I waited impatiently for the last and final gong...
But it seemed some life was left to be squeezed out from me...
But when least expected, the final gong struck, leaving me falling into the abyss..
Headlong I plunged, the fathoms cold and sinister...
But somewhere in the trench, some fireflies caught my sight...
They lit the path away to bliss where I would find my meaning...
Just when I thought, my path had ended, here I begin...
The new untrodden path awaits me, my heart laden with hope...
And Marching ahead I go, the explorer keen and sure...
So 'rest', my friend, u can wait, the journey is yet to begin...

In search of colour

Drab as i was, i flitted in a hurry,
I sought colour amidst my peers in a scurry..
I looked on in awe as they spread their wings, each an masterpiece...
Of the master artist of the yore..
If only i could steal some colour, i looked on in vain..
The dainty ones unaware of the sinister notions...
I tore of in the opposite direction, tears welled my eyes..
It wasn't so easy, to become so vibrant..
I cursed my critics, what were they thinking when they called me a bore..
Then off i dived into the calm ocean to dissolve in the waters..
It wasn't so easy, again my eyes met..
A riot of colours going hither and thither...
Omigosh! Classes or schools ! Of fish so vibrant..
They marched, or rather swam in colour coded straits...
I swam away sulking..colours were so depressing, i thought deep inside..
As i sprang from the water holding on to dear breath...
My spirit sank at the sights in the coast..

Humans, once my fellow men frolicked in the warm sands..
Basking in the sun's glory, sans the once revered clothing..
In all the nudity, the colours and hues so vibrant..
They challenged predecessors to find the ends of the spectrum..
No longer did i run for the pot of colours..
I realised it's well within me, the pot waiting to be unleashed..
Waiting for the one who can strike just right at the crux..
I looked above at the beaming rainbow, and drank in the sheer beauty..
In gratitude..

The final bell

She reclined in her arm chair, the spectacles hanging precariously..
The drapes hung loosely on her drooping shoulders and hips..
The long pendulous strikes of the grandfather clock, set in motion, a flash back..
And she traveled unwittingly into the maze of memories of the yonder..
The charm and poise with which she stood, commanded respect from all..
Decisions were balanced and crisp to core, naysayers went up in thin air..
Stolen glances and hushed comments always beckoned to the child in her..
The sprawling lawns and teenage hues kindled the desire in her..
Many a time she wished to step out of the cloak of honour, she was bestowed..
To laugh and guffaw and to shout and whistle..to her heart's content..
To run wide in glee, with arms outstretched, into the horizon afar..
To love without inhibitions and to care without forethought...

But neither did the bells tire not did the weary assistant to remind of her pending tasks..
With a do or die spirit, she marched along, nevertheless...
But now as the silence looms large filling the crevices and the vacuum..
She pines long for the long lost romances, the vanishing fragrance and the whispers of hope...
As the bell strikes the final toll, the spectacles fall off the limp frame...
Finally the soul can love uninhibited, laugh in mirth and rock the moon to sleep..

My rubies

I held the barbed wire gingerly…
In a foolish hope that my hand will be safe…
Just hold gently, no need to be scared…
Just then my arm was pulled by a force, i couldn't reckon..
The pain seared my heart, and my soul screamed in anguish…
The cool breeze tried drying my tears and drops of sweat..
My outpouring of sorrow and fret..
But the source was incessant, never to be stopped..
The blood, my blood shone on the barbed wire..
The clots thickened in time..
My rubies had been spilt out, without much ado..
I fought and cried desperately..
But now, entered a calm…
A quiescence, where the pain no longer held a place..
The calm spread into my soul and silenced my fears…
And rest i did at last, my rubies in my eyes…

Indulge

What if I didn't spell the love from my heart...
The intrigued lock eyes would have continued ceaseless...
If I didn't let myself be embraced in the warm hugs...
My heart would have continued thumping wild without peace...
If I didn't let my hands be held and felt safe...
The flush would have continued to wax and wane in hope...
If I didn't let my hair be stroked softly and tenderly..
The heavenly feel would have remained entrapped in poetry...
If I refrained from getting drenched in the downpour...
The pleasure of water on raw skin would be just a fantasy...
If I covered myself head to toe from the warm sun...
The surge of warmth and the cool breeze would be anonymous to me...
If I didn't allow myself to cry and laugh as it came...
The soul would long for a reprieve resulting in many rebirths...
If I didn't indulge, in everything as it came, raw and sweet...
The pleasures would remain hidden treasures unto my last breath...
So indulge, from within and in all vigour, never hold back....
As shyness and guilt are just marring the beautiful self within...

If I were a child again..

I will be the first to run into the rain, drenching myself to the core...
I will talk unabashed to all and sundry, my hearts thoughts,
After all it's but one life, no regrets whatsoever..
I will lie on the lap of my granny, hearing her narrate tales of her valour..
I will crouch near my mother, wondering how I played football in her womb..
I will sit open mouthed, hearing the wise words of my appa..
I shall suck on lollipops and sip ups not worrying about my tonsils..
I will have pillow fights with my brother and cousins, till the air is filled with cotton balls..
I shall ogle at the handsome stars and envy all the beauties out there...
I shall not mind giving a loud piece of my mind to all offenders who ask for it...
After all I'm generous, mind you..
I shall prance about in the dress of my choice, giving no heed to naysayers...
I shall try gulping the fog that attempts to engulf me, to taste how it feels..
I shall propose to the heartthrob of the moment, making terms and conditions very clear...
I shall learn and compose music to sing my poems...
I shall paint all the white walls with pictures from my heart...
I guess it is time for a rebirth, now in this life, here I go...
Gaga...

Twisted tale

The little girl looked on, at the cottony puffs of clouds,
As They glided lazily as if dipped in Holi colours,
Some a little to the further, streaked in blood, blood of the demon.
As narrated by her grandmother, the tales of the slayer of evil.
Garlanded with heads, and hands armed with weapons blood streaked.
For a moment, the little one wondered in surprise,
If she saw a glimpse of the goddess, in the narrator.
The raindrop rolled down, gathering dirt from the dusty leaves,
Made so by the galloping hooves that kicked up dust.
The equine army that marched, signalling the end of the festival.
And now the streets lay deserted, the air fragrant with petrichor.
The dark clouds heaved and lightning struck,
As if to strike home the truth, marred in the mire of rituals.
Blindly followed sans meaning, sans sense,
Somewhere, a laugh, a sarcastic one, echoed in the horizon,
Mocking at the narrator and the devoted listener.

Thupaaki

Deserted and discarded, the toy gun lay,
Covered in dust and grime, much toyed with play.
Enthused, the lad picked it up, gingerly lest it shot...
A milestone apart, lay a hamlet, slowly awaking from its slumber.
A whine arose in pitch and turned to a blood curdling cry,
Hooves pounded, kicking up dust, and the villain whipped them up.
Neighs ripped the air, the dawn in tatters, mercy thrown to the wolves.
The lad aimed, screwing his eye, at the heart of the villain.
The thupaaki shot the villain dead, sans a drop of blood.

The chugging train

The chug of the train, sends me back to days of yore,
When I sat cuddled and cross legged next to the window,
Munching on peanuts and balarama,
When the tales of amar chitra katha, enthused me,
When I was in bliss in reality without need for a virtual escape,
Not that there was one at the time,
When the coconut palms lining the paddy,
Looked so romantic in the rains,
Small boys in banian, pranced about in the rain,
Lemon candies and ginger candies sought by watery mouths,
When the malayali ladies looked beautiful in their kasavu saris,
And men elegant in their mundu,
And lamp lighting was an elaborate affair,
When power cuts were treasured times,
And chitrageethams and rangoli were more than enough for our racing hearts

The little me

She stood before me, a sullen face,
Rather she chose this face,
It would help to hide from the fears,
It would help mask the insecurity,
And as everyone said, she put up a bold face,
Things happened, much beyond her years,
She stood, a silent witness.
For years she battled the wars within,
But finally she gave away to smiles,
But yet a beautiful mask to the battles within.
Tis was better this way, why would the world care?

Happy wrinkles

As the dawn shed it's colours to the looming silhouettes...
As the velvety night sky gave way to orange hues...
As the early birds left in search for their breakfast..
The lone lass sat by her canoe, looking deep beyond the horizon..
With painted lips, dyed hair and masked wrinkles..she implored..
To the society which defied her aging.
As if grey hair and crow lines were a challenge to her dignity...
Somewhere deep down, she defied it all with sarcasm...
But the outer was calm, an uneasy calm...
Just as natural as the sun rose and buds bloomed...
Just as waves crashed and the nightingale sang...
Just as babies crooned and brides blushed...
So did she want to age naturally, grey and white...
For the wrinkles to stand out unopposed, for her lips to breathe pale and pink...
For the nature to paint her from its own palette of colours...
For the society to accept her in her own tender skin...

Before I die

I want to get splashed from head to toe in the colours of Holi...
I want to chase rabbits down and deep to their holes...
I want to feel the snow on my cheeks, hair and feet...
I want to board the polar express and witness the wonders of Christmas..
I want to go canoeing in the calm waters of the Venice...
I want to shout out my love from the mountain top and hear my echoes loud and clear...
I wish to express my hearts desires to my beloved folk...
I wish to seek forgiveness for all my faults trivial and big...
I want to scale the heights and watch the mist covered peaks in wonder...
I wish to surround myself with the love I deserve and cherish every moment there is...
So on and forth, I guess the list is, endless to speak, desires fathomless...
So on i go wish by wish, to cease when my call does come...

Fever down the ages

In the days of innocence, with suppressed glee and a breaking voice,
I announced my fever to my mom.
With a pride i enjoyed the rare privilege of being pampered to the core.
I chose to ignore the piling notes or the complaints of my brother.
As here i was, the little princess, being fed and sponged and what not.
With disdain i looked at the mercury drop and with it the added benefits.
With passing years and greying hairs here i am down with fever again.
But this time, the privileges rare and sought after.
But guilt a strong contender, as my kids walk about proclaiming their needs.
My waning immunity a question always subject to theoretical debates.
Among loved ones, who wish to see me stoic and robust.
Deep down i hide my anguish, of unmet needs and desires.
And i bury myself deeper and deeper into the warm depths of my blanket.
I nurse my child caressing and fondling and reassuring it of my profound love.
That iam my own nurturer and caretaker to the end.

Death vs life

Alas, a day will be borne, when you will forget me...
Into the shadows of oblivion, i may be cast.
The fragrances you adored, just a faded memory.
The laughs that rocked you, a faraway whisper,
And the touch of passion, just a feathery dream.
As the sand slips through endless time,
As things decay, slow and sure,
Memories shall fade far beyond.
But in my mind, they live on in vivid colours,
Dancing and prancing about in vibrant hues.
The smells, tastes and touch passionate and fragrant to the core.
Memories filled with frolic and mirth,
They will live on, fed and nurtured in the tender folds of my mind.

Gulmohar

From the summer's heat, sprang fiery blossoms,
Like soldiers from an angry womb.
Akin to unbridled passion riddling hearts in love,
In the backdrop of verdant green and azure skies.
Red flags sprang up in protest, the gulmohar steadfast in support…
Slogans raised and blood rushed in vivid hues of red.
Akin to the fresh blood strewn in tripe and war…
The woman in wedlock awaited draped in red,
Hair loose and in protest, the sari caressed the fallen blooms.
As she sat in wait beneath the gulmohar, livid in bloom.
One wondered if it's the goddess, incarnate awaiting justice.

Bait in wait

I waited till the time was right,
Till autumn would give away to spring,
I waited for the bud to bloom, to whisper the secret, held so dear.
I waited for the rains to stall, lest i catch an unwieldy cold.
I waited for the delayed train, oblivious of the little delights.
I waited for you to halt and sneak a peek at my pining eyes...
The dawn did rise, the sun did set as always from time untold.
The waves that came ever retreated tempting endlessly...
But here I stand long in wait for the morrow, that never shall come.
Better now than never, lest the wait turns out a bait.

Letting go

At first it was scary, and met with disbelief,
How could I? The faces, the situations.
The baggage grew, steady and heavy,
Dragging me in my trail, the horizon a blur.
They opined things, i 'should' be doing, of the right things in life.
No longer, did they seem any farther from wrong.
My heart had set forth, on a journey, hitherto unexplored.
Covered in vines and prickly bushes, intimidating the timid self.
Yet something tugged so hard, i had to relent,
And here i go, in baby steps, forsaking the vines.
Allowing myself to bleed and heal, my baggage getting lighter.
Letting go of loved and adored ones, who served as barnacles.
For my ship has set to sail, the journey of a thousand miles.
I have to go, the need is prime, naked in soul and body.
For tomorrow waits in all splendor, for the plunge, i must take.

Slow motion

Sometimes life unfolds as an art movie,
Classical are the scenes, enticing to senses,
The pulsing of the veins, the sweat drops of love,
The dew drop traversing the veins of the leaf,
The snail cruising along, slow and steady,
The mindful chewing of betel leaves by old granny,
The train chugging along, musical to my ear,
The hymns from the temple, flowing to my ears,
The slow demure looks, of the beauty in the train,
The wisps of hair that try in vain to hide the beauty,
The parted lips, that spoke desires,
The kid who snuggled close to his mother's bosom,
The innocence writ large in his eyes,
The beauty of life, slow yet sure,
To evoke the unspoken desires of the soul.

Rantings

To write, is a must, to vent the heart,
For the bleating of the sheep, the crooning of the pigeons,
Is unbearable to the ear, I'm drooling in insanity.
This me who is by heart an explorer, sought realms unconquered,
But surprised I'm as i realise, the virgin universe within me,
Hit by meteors, close to black holes,
I tread a minefield, tiptoeing in silence.
The very bodies around me have multiple personalities,
Or i guess, iam the schizophrenic,
Hallucinations, in all known senses, plague me and delight me.
The sorting is getting tedious as the tangles are more knotted,
But plod i shall nevertheless, easing a knot a day.
The death of feelings and birth of calm awaits me, with open hands.
I see the horizon, in a glimpse but i know for sure, it awaits.

Bougainvillea

The heat was scorching inside out,
Plants withered and so did souls,
Everywhere man scurried, to be under shade,
An ever elusive shade,
The canopies of trees were fast vanishing,
Rather banished from the scape,
The evil ways of the heat toyed with feeble minds,
Tempers and temperature both on rise,
Yet they bloomed unscathed by it all,
Draping mundane towers with a beauty beyond words,
As if lending hope to weary minds,
The riot of colours, cruising thorny ways,
They creeped over and covered the dismal sights,
Oh, soul, be resilient in the face of heat,
Resilience that is the bougainvillea.

Let the noose wait

Oh, soul, halt, let the noose wait,
Look around a bit, beyond the welling tears,
Beyond the flushed face and flood of thoughts,
What u feel, is not all that is...
There is hope beyond the chasm,
Oh, wait, do breathe, just a bit,
Just a bit more deep, feel the air, in your lungs,
Weren't you happy ever once in life,
Don't you remember the happy times,
No, my dear, they haven't gone,
True, they pained you, true you bled,
Yet it's over, the past is over,
You may sever ties, toxic ties and memories,
You are loved oh, soul, safe and secure,
Breathe, and sleep in new born bliss,
Say farewell to the noose, that hangs free,
Your days aren't over, your story awaits you,
Come forth, with your quill, write anew your story,
You have no one to prove yourself,
You need no one to validate you,
You are a gem, just because you live...
Tribute to dear Masood...my love and respect

The voice

Your voice lingers in my ears,
As you told you would come to see me off,
The little word fights, the twisted brows,
That transformed to chuckles and delight,
Your omnipresent smile and positive aura,
The way you touched numerous lives,
Empathetic to the core,
Little did I know that in the hours to follow,
You were chased by death, a violent chase,
That you would finally give to it,
That the bright smile would be erased once and for all,
But your voice lingers and smile too,
In the annals of my heart and all hearts you touched,
And memories come in waves, my friend,
Rest in peace, dear Rajeesh...

Fear of death

As you lay shrouded in white, amidst a pall of gloom,
I look beyond the veil of life to seek your vanishing soul,
A hundred questions nay thousand, flood my mind and choke me,
What about the roses I would give you on your birthday?
What about the loving words I would whisper in your ears?
What about the confessions I wished you would hear?
What about the long nights, we so cherished together?
What about the warm soup I would make for you?
What about the desires that you have yet to fulfill?
What about the trails we planned to go together?
What about the lonely nights you left me to cover?
As I implore you, and seek you back,
U smile at me, at my tears, as if to say,
It no longer matters, or rather never did matter,
That you would be, in the words I speak, the thoughts I think and the love I give.

The ghost

I was all ready to go, in wait for the auto,
I sat in my sitout in a rare moment of silence,
I wondered, how rare is silence in my life,
I long for it at times amidst chaos,
A soft breeze, sent the wind chimes ringing,
Amidst the soft swing of the chimes, I saw a flutter,
Must be a dream, I pinched myself,
Nay it was a dress, a white sari,
Slowly but surely, the one draped in it,
Came before me, white as snow,
Pale as death and soft as a whisper,
She sat before me, serene and silent,
Long slender fingers held the chair,
Beautiful tresses tumbled down her bosom,
A beauty beyond words, with sad eyes,
As I searched her face, for I know not what,
The horn of the auto, awakened me,
The lady was gone, in a wisp of thin air,
I was left, gaping mouthed and in wonder,
As I hurried to go, I slid my hand on her couch,
It was cool, cool as ice, yet dry as desert,
Unspoken words hung in the air, laden with sadness,
A mystery to the turmoil that suddenly lavished in my soul.

My Gowri

She is one little cracker of positive vibes,
Spreading joy wherever she sprints,
Even the ‘unlaughables’ are coerced into a laugh,
A hearty one that brings tears to one’s eyes,
At one time, she prances about like a kid in joy,
At another, she is engrossed in devouring books,
It’s not a single but many, the adventures we have had,
Through which I discerned, her love and sincerity,
She isn’t worth a dime, but a rare priceless gem,
My teacher unto the end, in ups and downs,
The wisdom that tumbles from her unhindered,
Puts me in awe, I realise the essence she beholds,
But the very next moment a prankster beyond doubt,
She leaves me befuddled, searching for answers,
Her chuckles fill my day, just as her gloom, hangs heavy,
I know not a dull moment with her all about.
I pray that the world is kind to her,
I pray that she reaches for her hearts desires,
And I pray that she remain the child she always is.

Do not change

You shower me with kisses, and are generous with hugs,
Like the pioneer of chipko, you hug me for dear life,
An earful of stories you fill me every hour,
Of lamentations and little worries, you skew your tiny face,
Loud laughter and mischievous smiles,
Light up your eyes and deepen your dimples,
I feel loved and honoured and blissful by you,
I hold on to these moments, as to dear life,
As a day may come when, kisses are awkward and hugs are rare,
As closed doors and long silences may become a norm,
Sigh! I shall deplore the moments, true as they may be,
Yet hold on to the love you once gave away so free,
And pray in my heart, that you may never change....

I see…I love

After all the years of wooing, and vying for the
heartstring of my beloved,
I realise that the well is always half empty, ever thirsty,
Exhausted, I see around for a respite, a glimmer,
What a fool I have been, the reservoirs of love brim around
me,
I see love in the breeze that wafts through my tresses,
In the beautiful trees that refresh my tired eyes,
In the raindrops that rejuvenate my skin and beyond,
I see love in the innocent chuckles of my kids,
There is love in the warm hugs I'm presented,
Love forms ripples in the lake within,
In the soft waves that caress my feet,
In the kind words and acts of strangers.
I see love in letting go of shame, guilt and perfection,
I see the beauty of love abundant in flawed humans,
In the tender feminine, I had been oblivious so long,
Hence, I'm now in love, deep love with the love of my life

Utopian world

A day shall come when I can err in life,
Without fear of persecution, knowing,
I will always be accepted, no matter,
The nature of my human errors,
For someone wise once said,
It's human to err and divine to forgive,
A day shall come, when the long queues to seek the truth,
In holy corridors dwindles to a drizzle,
And queues redirect to the temple within,
Therein lays the truth, of the soul
A day shall come when man realises that,
Behind the veil of weakling, lie an indomitable spirit and resilient,
And the resurrection of the phoenix is imminent,
A day shall come when man realises that mortar and cement can't give life,
To the most cherished values of love and forgiveness,
A day shall come when you and I realise the power of non violence,
That violence resonates with the unconscious spirit,
That violence can even be silent,
I wish I live to see that day,
When my kids live in the world of unconditional love
The utopian world of love,
Where one embraces the other as a whole,
As I am because you are....

I was guilty

I was guilty for not shoving aside the banana peels,
On the footpaths of the roads,
I was guilty of flinging sweet wrappers through, rail and bus windows,
I was guilty of stoic silence amidst groping in public buses,
I was guilty of not honoring myself against inappropriate advances of the 'stronger sex',
I was guilty of feigning ignorance to human crises,
When the solutions blared in my head,
I was guilty of skipping situations and people that needed my help,
Now here I stand, nowhere to go,
For death awaits, slow but sure,
Something in me, my conscience has come alive, no longer dead,
I speak my mind and write too, shedding the cloak of guilt,
Before the toll does come, let's do a deed,
To honor us and our kin.

God

I was told that you had to be feared,
That you had numerous names and forms,
That your tastes varied beyond measure.
That you like to be draped in red, silk?
And you liked to be decked in gold,
That one had to bathe, before seeing you,
As if bodily dirt is all that mattered.
That you didn't like menstruating girls,
For 'some reason' they were untouchable.
That sinning in wedlock would add to forego toxicity.
That one was always duty bound and had to forego pleasure.
That you disliked one indulging in bodily pleasures,
As if it made them less spiritual.
And that human being who errs even by mistake ought to be punished.
That you had a book which decided the,
Punishment for each sin, really?!!
That kids had to obey elders and live in hushed tones.
Though the orders went against their gut.
But now as I cross my youth, I realise,
How absurd was all that they told about you?
That you were a friend and lover without strings.
That you held a special love for women,
That you live unblemished in the child,
That you and fear are mutually exclusive.
That you live inside me and we are one.
That you whom I sought were seeking me after all.

Silence can kill..

I opened my mouth, yet all that came was a silence,
muted I was,
Oh, realise my pal, that silence is dangerous,
Silence in the face of abuse,
Silence amidst witnessing violence,
Propagating silence in budding minds,
Silence when numbers are tortured,
Silence when your loved ones are harmed,
Teaching kiddos that responding is dangerous,
Teaching em' that silence can help u get away in life,
Halt, and realise your folly, Oh, great parents and
teachers,
For thou art breeding a generation of bullies and
murderers,
Insensitive to the hordes of innocent souls,
Akin to cold and hard boulders,
No longer can they be called your breed,
Arise, awake and teach them to respond,
So that the tender bud of love isn't trampled.

For whom should I wait

To spend the night, counting stars,
To cuddle beneath the warm blankets,
To count the waves kissing the shore,
To feel the warmth of the bonfire,
The wait's been long, o! My pal,
I judge thy not, yet my gut doth feel,
My wait has been futile, for the truth is,
That Im a mere mortal, wearing my body,
For this lifetime that's given,
For you too are a mortal and so am I.
Wat do you have to give in to me,
To hold me waiting longer,
Though a mere mortal, my desires know no bounds,
And hence I go forth, lone in my trail,
Leaving you, glimmers, if ever you want,
If ever the mortal you, thinks otherwise.

Lend me your shoulder

I will not utter a word, lest you go awry,
I have a zillion things running within me,
A race that sees no end, win or loss,
How can I tell you what I think,
When the language of my eyes and words are alien to you.
When a word or even a gesture can evoke fuming embers,
Let me run away from the world of aliens,
To a known home, a shoulder to cry upon,
To see through my silence, and embrace the meaning,
Where the silence can comfort, not kill,
Where I can sleep in peace, not worrying about the
morrow.
When the twilight and gentle breeze hold answers,
To questions alien to humankind,
I wish to disappear once and for all,
Into the bliss that is your presence.

You are precious

I quarrelled with you over petty matters,
Not knowing your precious worth.
Over unkempt clothes and house,
Over dishes and laundry and the mundane.
Over flab and lazy couch days.
It's time to ask forgiveness for the darts of hurt.
That you live still makes you one of a kind,
Oh! precious chosen one!
I harboured dissent over the restraints,
Over my self proclaimed freedom,
I despised being 'looked down upon'
As a child yet to grow,
I wished to break the unseen chains,
You seem to bind me in,
Knowing little that the chains were my own doing,
That I'm free of all thoughts, mine and yours,
That my will is unbound in past, present and ever.
I ask for forgiveness for the plain dissent,
I set you free of doubt and hate,
I know how precious you are, for you live and you breathe.

I was born in you, my clothes for good,
Oft, I despised the many aspects,
Comparing and contrasting with the greener grass,
I wondered if I could be someone else,
Yet forgetting how long and strong,
You stood by me in moments of strife and pain.
Of how you withstood all insults yet arose every morning,
With a faith, unwavering and devoted,
I ask for forgiveness, my dear body,
I accept you in whole, wholesome that you are.
I ask for forgiveness and bow in gratitude for all that you are.
Precious you are beyond words, treasured you will always be.
Be with me as I awake each morning that I'm destined to.

Love beyond grief

She was elated but, in grief,
He had confessed his love for her.
The sudden downpour and the bright rainbow,
Added surrealism to the romantic event.
Her heart raced in the cage, longing for freedom.
Her soul wished to scale mountains, her lover's hand in hers.
She wished to leap into his arms and be held so for ever.
The goosebumps, the delight and sparkle were followed,
By immeasurable grief and sorrow,
As she realised her handicap and it's crippling effect.
The body couldn't keep to the pace of the soul.
She succumbed in relief into sturdy arms...
Arms that reassured her that true love existed and it was no longer fiction.
She could just let go of it all, yet have it all back together in whole...

Gratitude

The moon played hide and seek among the dark clouds...
The waves caressed my tired feet and implored me to go forth..into the depths..
Dogs played, barking and frolicking in the white sand..
My pale hands beneath the waters, showed clearly the twist of my destiny..
In a world of wellwishers and critics alike, I have begun hearing my voice..
No longer strangled, but clear and steady, no longer feeble but strong and loud..
I seek to pleasure myself with the warmth of my soulmates.
The laughter that echoes through the darkness of the night..
The memories of this day shall last forever...
Ode to the souls who made my day and are here to stay...

Rebirth

I glided in the canoe, in the midst of still waters..
Far afar from the madding crowd..
Oblivious to the numerous demands of time and people..
I travelled aeons to the fields where the heather was in full bloom..
Tulips and daffodils smiled at me in innocent mirth..
The sun warmed my cold and moist cheeks and rid the chill..
Love wrapped me in its folds, gentle, caressing and warm..
Non judgmental, and embracing me in full with all my idiosyncrasies and idiocity..
The freckles, hump and squint, all so valuable now, prized possessions..
I'm so far from embattled minds that sucked my spirit...
And enthralled in the ecstasy of the moment...
I wish it would all last and dissolve me into the essence of it all..
Never do I wish to vacillate between the tentacles of moodswings...
But I guess, the pain is what makes love endearing and priceless...
So here I go again..Sayonara...